* BIRTHDAY CARDS ✫ CROSSWORDS ☾

COLORING PICTURES ✳ DOT-TO-DOT PICTURES ✫

GET-WELL CARDS

☾ HIDDEN PICTURES *

MATCHING PICTURES

MAZES ✳ WORD SEARHCES ☾ *

Reproducible Activities for preschool to sixth grade

ARRIVAL ACTIVITIES

from A to Z

Things to Do When the First Child Arrives

Abingdon Press

Arrival Activities from A to Z

98 99 00 01 02 03 04 05 06 07 — 10 9 8 7 6 5 4 3 2 1

MANUFACTURED IN THE UNITED STATES OF AMERICA

CONTENTS

3

Introduction

It's Sunday morning and you are getting ready for your class. As you are busy setting up the Sunday school lesson, does:

- the pastor's son come to class thirty minutes early?
- a woman from the Dorcas class leave her granddaughter while she goes to the coffee fellowship?
- another Sunday school teacher send her twins to your class so she can get her own classroom ready?

Then **Arrival Activities from A to Z** can help you!

Involve your children in the day's lesson as soon as they walk in the door with:

- an activity that relates to the Bible story for the day,
- a greeting card for the children to decorate and send, or
- a simple coloring picture.

Photocopy as many copies as you need for your children. A symbol on each page will tell you what age level will enjoy the activity.

Preschool

Younger Elementary

Older Elementary

AbrAHam

Angels

God's Promise to Abraham

Directions: Have the children follow the arrows to find the promises God made to Abraham. Check the answer by reading Genesis 12:2.

START HERE

I

will   a

make

you   you,   I

will   make   that   be   great

bless   so   and

of   and   you

name   a

blessing.

will

great,

nation,

God's Covenant With Abraham

Directions: Have the children cross out the OT's (Old Testament) to read the words from Genesis that tell about God's covenant with Abraham. Read Genesis 12:2 and Genesis 17:7.

IOT WIOTLL MAOTKEOT
OOTF YOOTUOT AOT
GREOTAOTT NAOTTIOTOOTN,
AOTND IOT WIOTLL BLEOTSS
YOOTUOT, AOTND MAOTKEOT
YOOTUOTR NAOTMEOT
GREOTAOTT, SOOT THAOTT
YOOTUOT WIOTLL BEOT AOT
BLEOTSSIOTNG... IOT WIOTLL
EOTSTAOTBLIOTSH MY
COOTVEOTNAOTNT
BEOTTWEOTEOTN MEOT
AOTND YOOTUOT, AOTND
YOOTUOTR OOTFFSPRIOTNG
AOTFTEOTR YOOTUOT.

Genesis 12:2; 17:7

Angels Angels

Directions: Have the children read each of the Scriptures listed below to find out what the Bible says about angels. Then have the children find the matching answer under the angels list.

It was the angel Gabriel who brought the good news about Jesus' birth to Mary and to Joseph. There are many other references to angels in Scripture. What do angels do? Find some answers in your Bible. Then match the references with what you learn from them. Remember, some references will have more than one answer!

SCRIPTURES	ANGELS
_____ Exodus 23:20	a. bring good news
_____ Psalm 91:11	b. help people not to be afraid
_____ Matthew 1:20	c. help people know what God wants them to do
_____ Matthew 4:11	
_____ Matthew 28:1-6a	d. rejoice when sinners repent
_____ Luke 1:26-31	e. give strength in time of trouble
_____ Luke 2:8-10	f. assure people that they are safe
_____ Luke 15:10	g. free people from imprisonment
_____ Luke 22:42-43	h. lead people where God wants them to go
_____ Acts 8:26-27a	
_____ Acts 10:3	i. guard over God's people
_____ Acts 5:17-20	j. care for Jesus (or us)
_____ Acts 27:23-25	

Good News! Mary will have a baby.

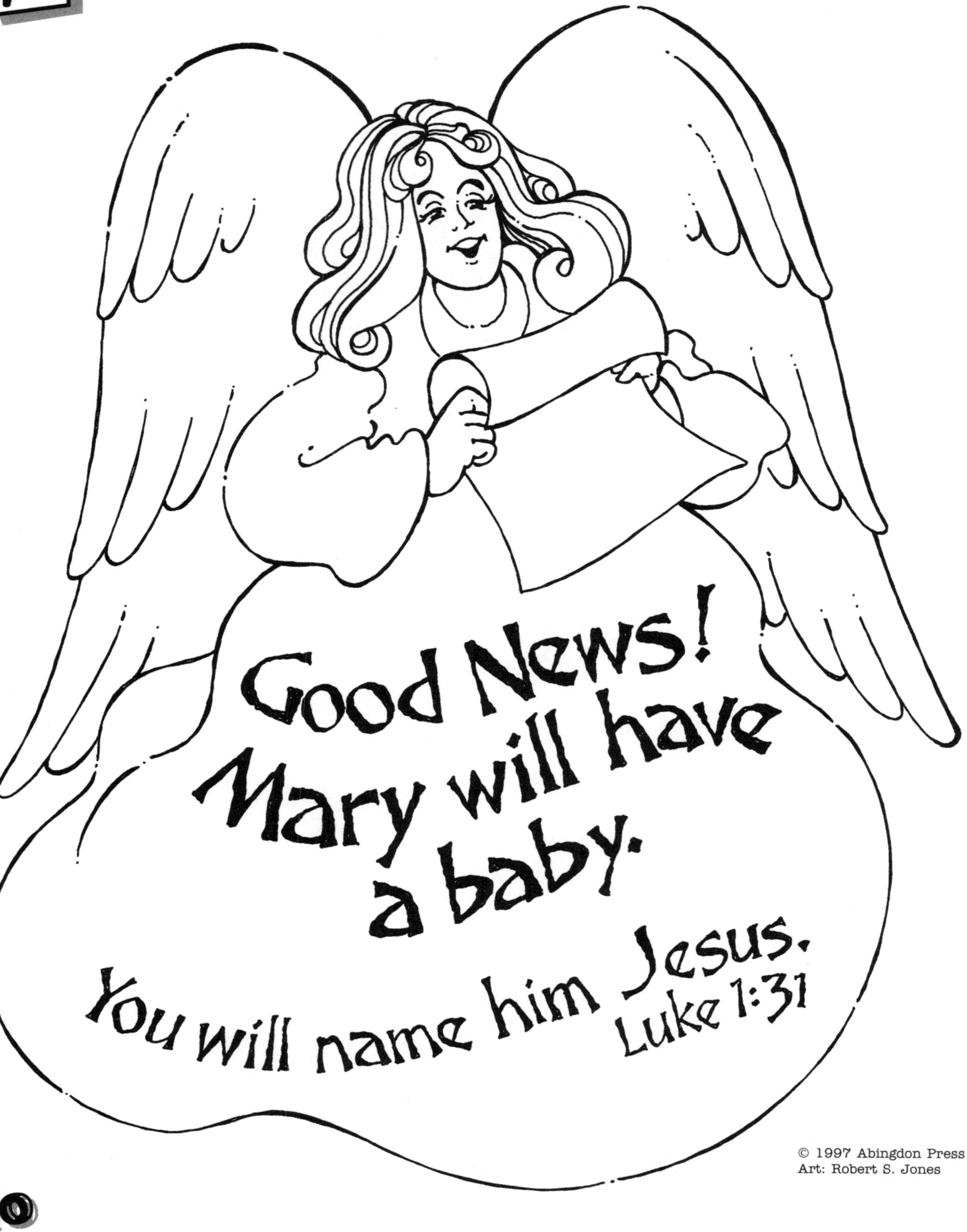

You will name him Jesus. Luke 1:31

Bible

Old Testament
Fill in the missing names

New Testament
Fill in the missing names

Old Testament

Directions: Have the children use the contents pages of their Bibles to help them fill in the missing names of Old Testament books.

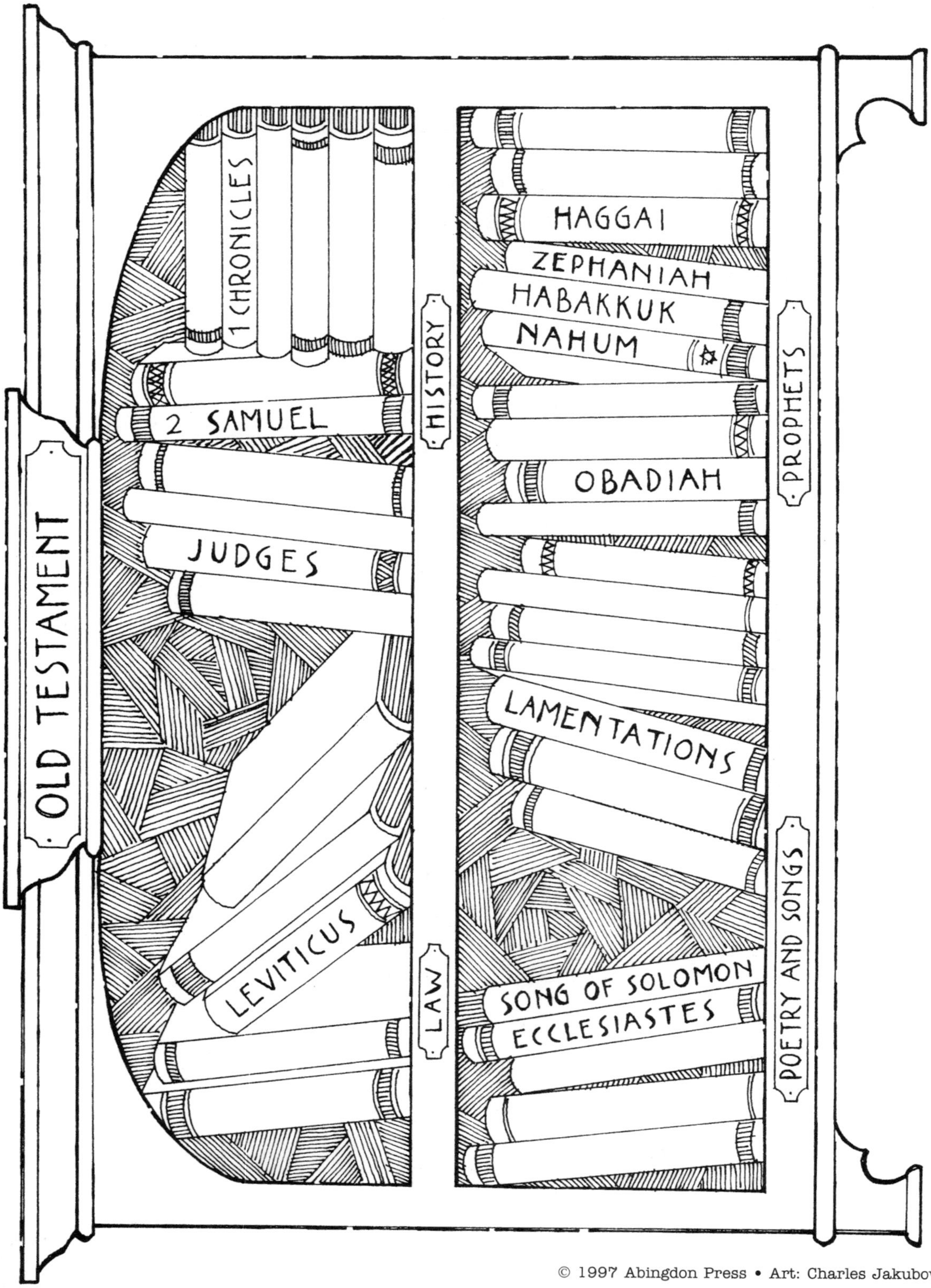

OLD TESTAMENT

HISTORY

PROPHETS

LAW

POETRY AND SONGS

1 CHRONICLES

2 SAMUEL

JUDGES

LEVITICUS

HAGGAI

ZEPHANIAH

HABAKKUK

NAHUM

OBADIAH

LAMENTATIONS

SONG OF SOLOMON

ECCLESIASTES

New Testament

Directions: Have the children use the contents pages of their Bibles to help them fill in the missing names of New Testament books.

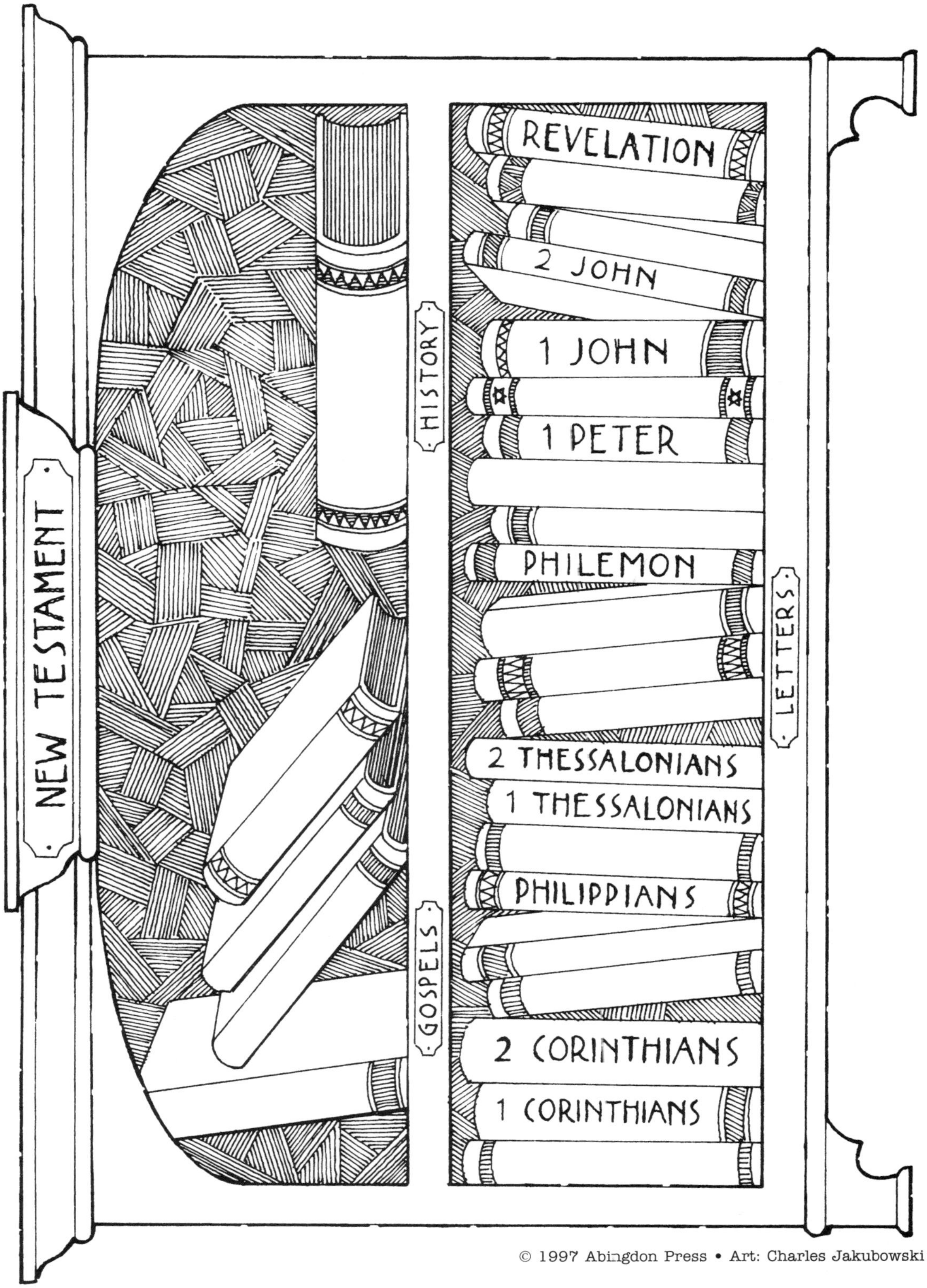

NEW TESTAMENT

GOSPELS

HISTORY

LETTERS

REVELATION

2 JOHN

1 JOHN

1 PETER

PHILEMON

2 THESSALONIANS

1 THESSALONIANS

PHILIPPIANS

2 CORINTHIANS

1 CORINTHIANS

Christmas

CrEATioN

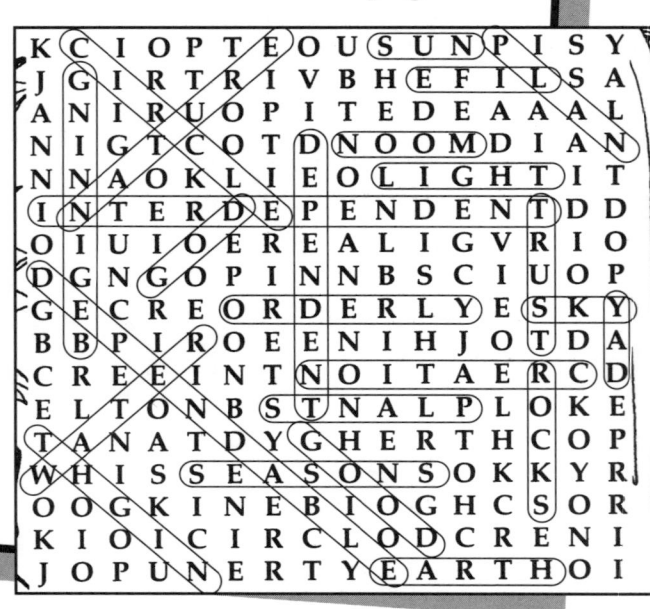

Jesus Is Born

Directions: Photocopy and cut apart at least two sets of the pictures. Encourage the children to match the pictures, or use the pictures to play a concentration game with the children. Turn all the pictures face down.

Have a child turn over one picture. Then have the child try to turn over the matching picture. If the picture matches, leave both pictures face up. If the picture does not match, turn the picture face down again. Continue until the child has found all the matches.

15

Where's Baby Jesus?

Directions: Have the children find baby Jesus in the picture. Encourage the children to draw a circle around baby Jesus.

Find Baby Jesus

Baby Jesus

Poinsettia

Directions: Let the children decorate the picture of the poinsettia with crayons or markers. Tell the children that the poinsettia is a flower that is often used for decoration at Christmastime.

The Promise

Directions: Have the children write the letter that each dove is carrying on the space with the matching number.

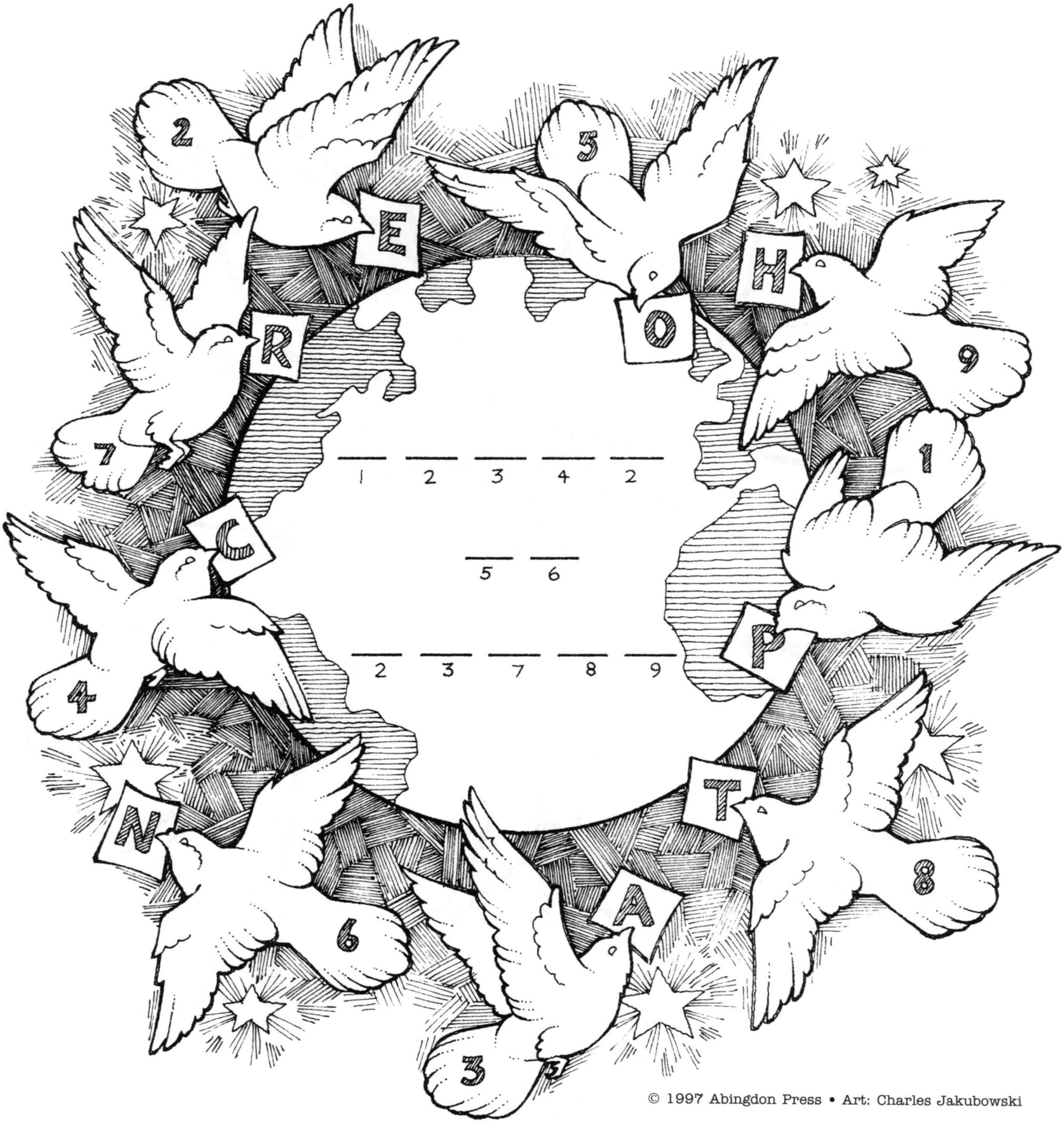

```
__  __  __  __  __
 1   2   3   4   2

    __  __
     5   6

__  __  __  __  __
 2   3   7   8   9
```

New Life in God's Creation

Directions: Photocopy and cut apart at least two sets of the pictures. Encourage the children to match the pictures of the baby creatures, seeds, and eggs with the pictures of what the creatures and plants become.

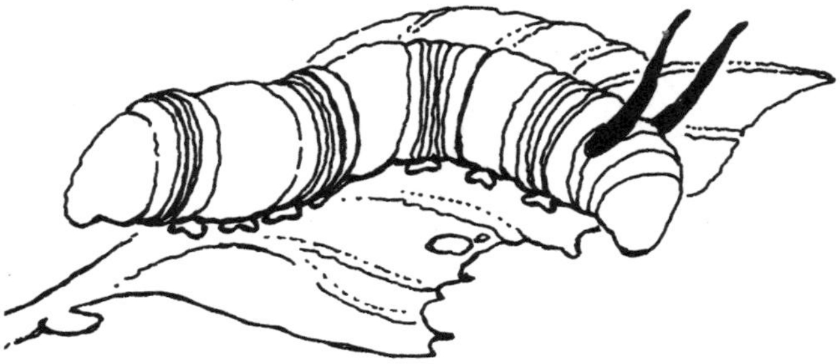

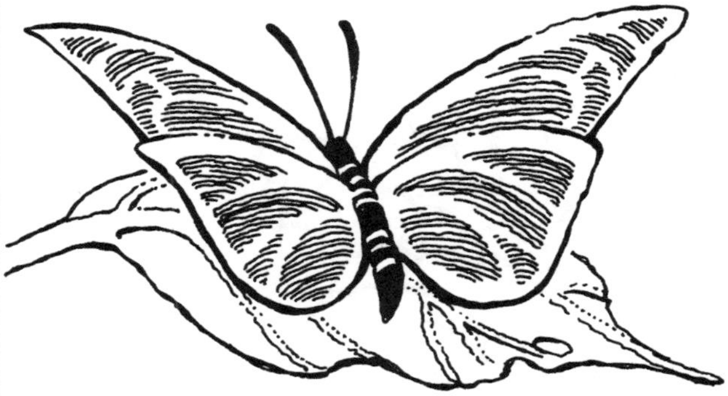

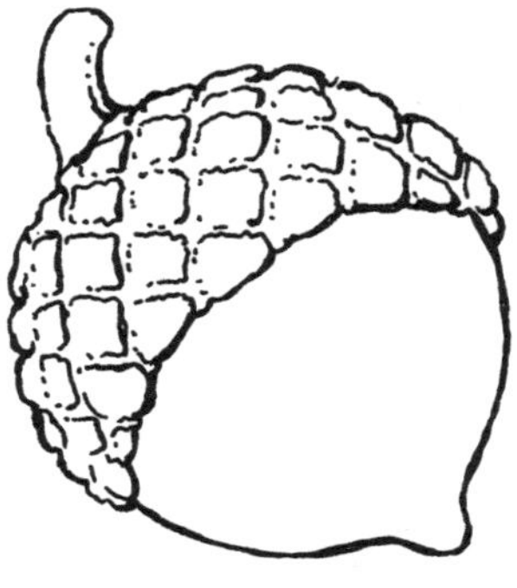

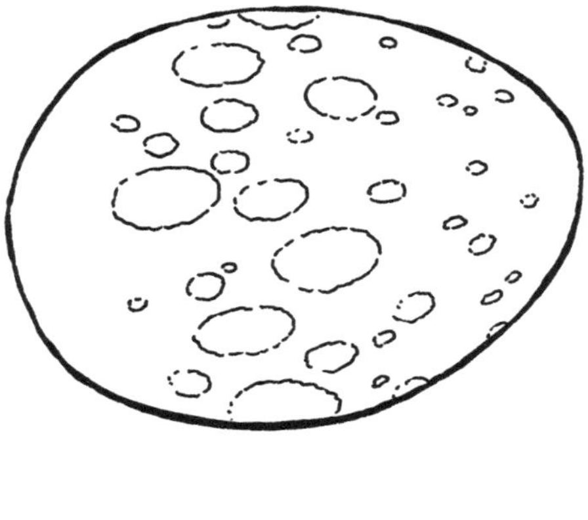

19

Sea Creatures

Directions: Photocopy and cut apart at least two sets of the pictures.
Encourage the children to match the pictures.

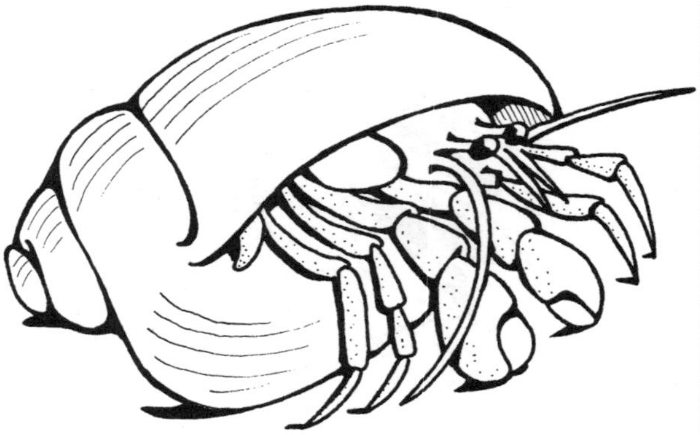

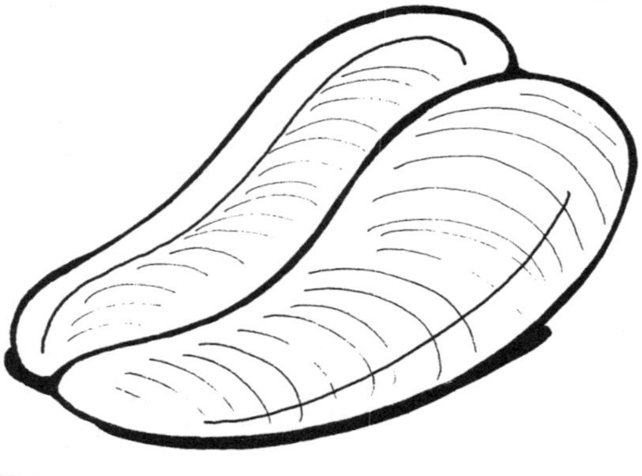

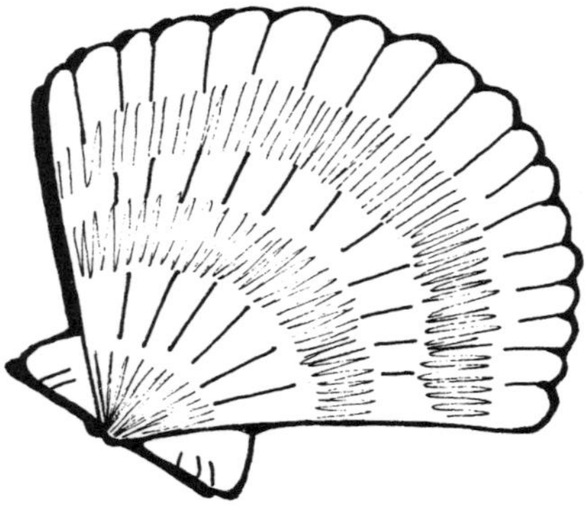

Animal Homes

Directions: Have the children follow the path from each animal to the
animal's home. Use a different color for each animal.

Path goes
under bridges

under
bridge

under
bridge

under
bridge

Path goes
under bridges

God's Creation

Directions: Have the children find the words printed at the top of the picture.

Animals Beginning Circle Creation Day Dependable
Dependent Earth God Good Interdependent Life Light
Moon Nature Night Orderly Plan Plants Rocks
Seasons Seed Sky Sun Trust Water

How many words that describe God's creation can you find in the word search?

```
K C I O P T E O U S U N P I S Y
J G I R T R I V B H E F I L S A
A N I R U O P I T E D E A A A L
N I G T C O T D N O O M D I A N
N N A O K L I E O L I G H T I T
I N T E R D E P E N D E N T D D
O I U I O E R E A L I G V R I O
D G N G O P I N N B S C I U O P
G E C R E O R D E R L Y E S K Y
B B P I R O E E N I H J O T D A
C R E E I N T N O I T A E R C D
E L T O N B S T N A L P L O K E
T A N A T D Y G H E R T H C O P
W H I S S E A S O N S O K K Y R
O O G K I N E B I O G H C S O R
K I O I C I R C L O D C R E N I
J O P U N E R T Y E A R T H O I
```

Daniel

David

Disciples

Tales From the Script

Directions: Have the children find the letter that is missing from the alphabet in each line. Write the correct letter in the space at the bottom of the page to complete the Bible verse.

1) A B C D E F G I J K L M N O P Q R S T U V W X Y Z
2) A B C D F G H I J K L M N O P Q R S T U V W X Y Z
3) A B C D E F G I J K L M N O P Q R S T U V W X Y Z
4) B C D E F G H I J K L M N O P Q R S T U V W X Y Z
5) A B C E F G H I J K L M N O P Q R S T U V W X Y Z
6) A B C D E F G H I J K L M N O P Q R S U V W X Y Z
7) A B C D E F G H I J K L M N O P Q S T U V W X Y Z
8) A B C D E F G H I J K L M N O P Q R S T V W X Y Z
9) A B C D E F G H I J K L M N O P Q R T U V W X Y Z
10) A B C D E F G H I J K L M N O P Q R S U V W X Y Z
11) A B C D F G H I J K L M N O P Q R S T U V W X Y Z
12) A B C E F G H I J K L M N O P Q R S T U V W X Y Z
13) A B C D E F G H J K L M N O P Q R S T U V W X Y Z
14) A B C D E F G H I J K L M O P Q R S T U V W X Y Z
15) A B C D E F G I J K L M N O P Q R S T U V W X Y Z
16) A B C D E F G H J K L M N O P Q R S T U V W X Y Z
17) A B C D E F G H I J K L M N O P Q R T U V W X Y Z
18) A B C D E F H I J K L M N O P Q R S T U V W X Y Z
19) A B C D E F G H I J K L M N P Q R S T U V W X Y Z
20) A B C E F G H I J K L M N O P Q R S T U V W X Y Z

Daniel was taken up out of the den, and no kind of harm was found on him, because

1 2   3 4 5   6 7 8 9 10 11 12
_____
13 14   15 16 17   18 19 20 .

Daniel 6:23b

Write a post card to Daniel. Tell him about a time when you were afraid. Tell him what it was like for you when you tried to trust God.

Purrr.

David the Shepherd

Directions: Have the children decorate the picture with crayons or markers.
Let the children connect the dashes to complete David's belt.

Look at the Heart

Directions: Have the children cross out all the X's, Q's, and Z's to complete the Bible verse. Write the verse on the line below the puzzle.

```
X T Q X Z Q H Q Z X Q X E
L Q X Z X Z Q X O X Q R Z
Q Z Q D Z X Q X X Q L X Q
Z O Z X Q O Q Z K X Q Z X
S X Q O Z Q X N Q Z X Q T
Z X H X X Q Z E X Q Z H X
Z E Q A X X Z R Z Q T Q Z
```

_____.

1 Samuel 16:7

Fishing for People

Directions: Have the children connect the dots to see the completed picture.

Go and Make Disciples

Directions: Have the children follow the path to complete the Bible verse. Each time the children come to a letter in a circle, write the letter on the next blank line in the verse.

Go therefore and make disciples of all nations, _ _ p _ _ _ _ i _ _
them in the _ _ m _ of the _ _ t _ _ r and of the _ _ n and of
the _ _ _ _ _ _ _ _ r _ _ , and _ _ _ _ c _ _ n _ them to
_ _ e _ everything that I have c _ _ _ _ a _ _ _ _ d you. And
remember, I am _ i _ _ _ _ _ always.

Matthew 28:19-20

© 1996 Cokesbury • Art: Larry Rollins

ELijah

Elijah's God
Word search
1 Kings 18:18, 20, 22, 23, 25, 29, 31-32, 33, 38, 39

EzrA

Ezra's Trip
Maze
Ezra 1:1-7

Ezra Reads God's Law
Word puzzle
Nehemiah 9:1-2

Elijah's God

Directions: Have the children use their Bibles to complete the story about Elijah's God.
Have the children find each of the words written in the blanks in the word search.

Elijah's God

Elijah said, "You have forsaken the _____ of the Lord and followed the Baals." (1 Kings 18:18c)

Ahab assembled the prophets at Mount _____. (1 Kings 18:20)

_____ said, "I, even I only, am left a prophet of the Lord." (1 Kings 18:22)

Elijah and the prophets of Baal agreed that each would build an altar, but would put no _____ to it. (1 Kings 18:23)

Elijah told the prophets of _____ to go first. (1 Kings 18:25)

When the prophets of Baal cried to their gods, there was no _____, no _____, and no _____. (1 Kings 18:29)

Elijah built an altar with _____ stones. (1 Kings 18:31-32)

Elijah told the people to pour _____ on the offering and on the wood on the altar. (1 Kings 18:33)

When Elijah prayed, the fire of the Lord fell and consumed the burnt _____, the _____, the _____, the _____, and even the _____ in the trench. (1 Kings 18:38)

The people declared, "The Lord indeed is _____." (1 Kings 18:39)

```
V O C H C U P K N J L V T R
R R E T A W I L O K W O O D
J H A W R O N A H I N I F P
S T N E M D N A M M O C F S
S H S L E I J B D O H E E E
R T W V L I O D U I N R R N
J K E E L I O P S U T Y I O
F I R E O G W A T E R O N T
O E S N O P S E R O N I G S
```

Ezra's Trip

Directions: Have the children follow the path from Ezra and his friends to Jerusalem.

Jerusalem

© 1995 Cokesbury • Art: Benton Mahan

Ezra Reads God's Law

Directions: Have the children add each set of numbers. Then have the children write the letters that are written over a set of numbers that add up to 24 on the lines below.

WORD PUZZLE

When Ezra read the words from God's law aloud, the people began to cry. They knew they had not obeyed God's law, and they were sad.

Several days later, on the twenty-fourth day of the month, the people did something instead of just crying because they had disobeyed God. Find out what they did by completing this number puzzle.

On the lines below write the letters that are written over a set of numbers that add up to 24.

C	V	O	N	A	F
12	12	23	22	21	11
12	3	1	2	13	13

W	E	X	S	S	K
16	15	2	10	8	21
6	9	24	14	16	6

M	E	D	T	B	H
1	13	21	19	15	17
21	11	3	5	8	7

G	E	P	I	T	R
6	16	10	13	21	3
21	8	23	11	21	21

S	I	J	N	U	S
14	2	8	24	13	7
10	22	19	0	16	17

_ _ _ _ _ _ _ _ _ _ _

_ _ _ _ _

_ _ _ _ _.

 Read Nehemiah 9:1-2 to check your answer.

Feeding the 5000

Loaves and Fishes
Hidden picture
John 6:1-14

Forgiving Father

The Forgiving Father
Maze
Luke 15:11-24

Pigs Pigs Pigs
Coloring picture
Luke 15:11-24

Loaves and Fishes

Directions: Have the children find 5 loaves and 2 fish in the picture of Jesus feeding the 5000.

loaf

fish

The Forgiving Father

Directions: Have the children trace the path beginning when the younger son left his father and ending when he returned home to his father.

© 1994 Cokesbury • Jack Kershner

Pigs Pigs Pigs

Directions: Let the children decorate the picture with crayons or markers.

Get-well Cards

Get Well Soon
Coloring card

Sing a Happy Song
Coloring card

Golden Rule

The Golden Rule
Happy gram
Matthew 7:12

Find the Sheep
Word game
Luke 6:31

Good Samaritan

Good Samaritan
Crossword puzzle
Luke 10:25-37

Answers—page 42

37

Get Well Soon

Directions: Let the children color the get-well cards. Send the cards to persons in your church who are in the hospital.

© 1998 Abingdon Press • Art: Robert S. Jones

Sing a Happy Song

Directions: Let the children color the get-well cards. Send the cards to persons in your church who are in the hospital.

The Golden Rule

Directions: Write the child's name in the space provided. Let the children decorate the happy grams with gold or yellow crayons or markers.

is **kind to others**

Do for others what you want them to do for you. Matthew 7:12 *Good News Bible*

40

Find the Sheep

Directions: Have the children find the sheep that has the item under each blank. Copy the letter on that sheep in the blank to discover the Bible message.

Luke 6:31

Good Samaritan

Directions: Have the children read Luke 10:25-37 to find the answers to the crossword puzzle.

Across

2. The story of the good Samaritan is found in the Book of _____.
5. A person from Samaria.
7. Jesus told this parable to answer the question, "Who is my _____?"
8. A religious leader who led worship in the Temple.
9. The occupation of the man who asked Jesus a question.

Down

1. The people who attacked the traveler on the road.
2. A Temple worker who helped the priests.
3. Two of these coins were given to the innkeeper.
4. The type of story Jesus told.
6. The place where the Samaritan took the wounded traveler.
9. A strong, caring feeling.

Happy Birthday

Happy Birthday
Coloring page

Holy Week

I Remember!
Crossword puzzle

Answers—page 45

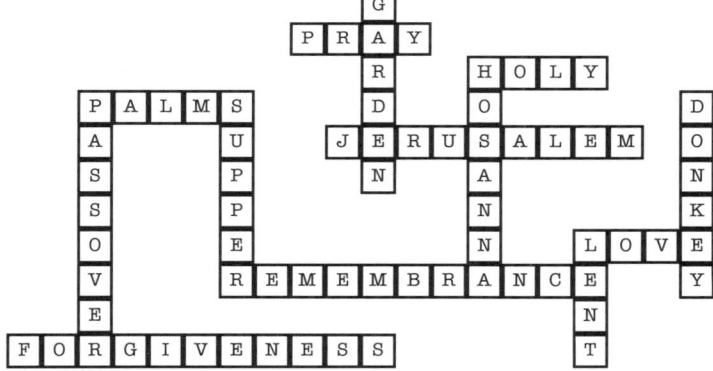

Happy Birthday

Directions: Let the children decorate the picture with crayons or markers. Give the picture to a child on her or his birthday, or let the children decorate several pictures to give to church friends on their birthdays.

It's your special day!

Happy Birthday!

I Remember!

Directions: Have the children answer the questions to complete the crossword puzzle.

Across

2. Jesus went to the garden of Gethsemane to _____.
3. Jesus' last week on earth is called _____ Week.
4. As Jesus rode into Jerusalem the people waved _____.
7. Jesus went to the city of _____ to celebrate Passover with his disciples.
8. The cross is a sign of God's _____ for us.
9. On Holy Thursday, Jesus blessed the bread and gave it to his disciples, saying, "Do this in _____ of me."
10. God offers us _____ of our sins.

Down

1. Jesus prayed in the _____ of Gethsemane while his disciples slept.
3. When Jesus rode into Jerusalem the people shouted _____.
4. In the upper room, Jesus shared the _____ meal with his disciples.
5. At the Last _____ , Jesus gave us a way to remember him.
6. Jesus rode a _____ into Jerusalem.
8. _____ is a special season of the Christian year that begins on Ash Wednesday and ends with Easter.

Isaiah

Isaiah the Prophet

Coloring page
Isaiah 1:1—66:24

Isaiah the Prophet

Directions: Let the children decorate the picture with crayons or markers.

© 1998 Abingdon Press • Art: Robert S. Jones

Jeremiah

Jesus

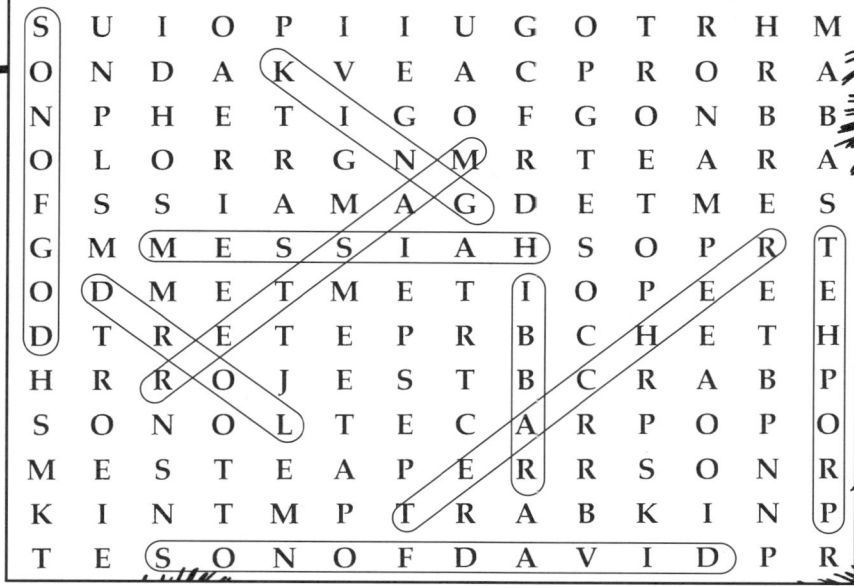

Jonah

Which Way Did He Go?
Maze
Jonah 1:1—4:11

Joseph

Joseph's Coat
Coloring page
Genesis 1:30; 25:30; 30:32; Exodus 15:22; 39:2;
Numbers 4:12; Leviticus 13:32; Proverbs 20:29;
Psalm 23:1-2; Mark 6:38-39; Acts 1:10; 16:14

Find Joseph's Brothers
Hidden picture
Genesis 42:1-13

Jeremiah

Directions: Have the children mark out all the B's, F's, K's, P's, U's, and W's. Then write the letters that are left on the line to discover what Jeremiah learned.

Jeremiah kept trying to tell people what God wanted them to hear, but . . .

☐ he was ignored when he spoke,

☐ his scroll was cut into pieces and burned,

☐ he was put in prison,

☐ he was abandoned in a muddy well.

But Jeremiah was faithful. He kept delivering the message God told him to deliver. Complete the cross out puzzle to discover an important lesson we learn from Jeremiah's experience.

Mark out all the **B**'s, **F**'s, **K**'s, **P**'s, **U**'s, and **W**'s.

Write the letters that are left on the line to discover what Jeremiah learned.

```
I  F  U  B  T  K  I  U  W  F  K  S
F  U  W  N  K  U  F  B  O  F  B  W
T  E  K  F  B  P  A  W  B  W  K  S
K  F  B  Y  B  F  T  P  U  W  O  U
F  B  K  P  D  W  E  F  B  L  F  B
I  P  B  B  V  E  P  U  B  F  W  U
R  B  U  K  W  G  B  F  K  O  F  P
P  K  D  K  B  F  S  F  P  M  F  W
E  K  F  B  S  K  U  W  B  S  W  A
B  F  K  P  U  W  B  K  G  F  B  E
```

_____ _____ _____

_____ , _____ _____

Jesus Is Risen

Directions: Let the children decorate the picture with crayons or markers.

Jesus is risen

Jesus Loves

Directions: Write the child's name in the space provided. Let the children decorate the picture with crayons or markers.

Jesus loves

What Did Jesus Learn?

Directions: Let the children look up the Scriptures listed in numbers 1-11.
Have the children find the matching answers in the right hand column.

Jesus learned the Scriptures of our Old Testament when he went to school at the synagogue. Match each Bible verse in the left column with what Jesus learned when he studied that verse at school.

____ 1. Deuteronomy 6:4-5

____ 2. Psalm 23:1

____ 3. Jeremiah 7:23

____ 4. Exodus 20:1-17

____ 5. Psalm 100:3

____ 6. Psalm 34:1

____ 7. Isaiah 61:1

____ 8. Psalm 95:6

____ 9. Deuteronomy 8:3b

____ 10. Psalm 91:14-15

____ 11. Deuteronomy 6:16

A. The Ten Commandments

B. Obey God's voice, and God will be your God, and you will be God's people.

C. Love God with your whole heart and with all your soul and might.

D. Bless and praise the Lord all the time.

E. Worship God.

F. God made us and we belong to God.

G. One does not live by bread alone, but by the words of God.

H. The Spirit of the Lord is upon me to bring good news.

I. God will take care of us like a shepherd takes care of the sheep.

J. God will protect and be with those who love God.

K. Do not test God.

Have you learned in Sunday school some of the same things Jesus learned in school at the synagogue?
Put a check mark beside each of the learnings that are important to you as a child of God.

Jesus Knew

Directions: Have the children follow the directions on the pictograph to discover the phrase, "Jesus knew God was with him."

[jeep] minus **ep** plus **S** plus **+** minus **pl**

[shirt with tag] **T** plus [hat]

[traffic light GO] plus [door] minus **oor** **Was**

[wind/dust] minus **nd** plus **Th**

[mountain] minus **ill** plus [clock] minus **t** and **e.**

Names for Jesus

Directions: Have the children look up the Bible verse to find nine names for Jesus. Then find the names in the word search.

Names for Jesus

When people met Jesus, their lives were changed. Often they called Jesus by a special name to describe how Jesus had affected their lives.

Can you find nine names for Jesus in the letters below? Use your Bible to find the names to look for.

Matthew 8:2   Luke 7:16   Matthew 9:27
Matthew 16:16   Matthew 8:29   Mark 9:5
Mark 4:38   Luke 19:38   Luke 5:5

```
S U I O P I I U G O T R H M
O N D A K V E A C P R O R A
N P H E T I G O F G O N B B
O L O R R G N M R T E A R A
F S S I A M A G D E T M E S
G M M E S S I A H S O P R T
O D M E T M E T I O P E E E
D T R E T E P R B C H E T H
H R R O J E S T B C R A B P
S O N O L T E C A R P O P O
M E S T E A P E R R S O N R
K I N T M P T R A B K I N P
T E S O N O F D A V I D P R
```

Which Way Did He Go?

Directions: Have the children start at the arrow to follow Jonah's path from Joppa to Nineveh. Direct the children to answer the questions they find along the way.

A storm/bad sailing threatened the boat.

Jonah decided to go to Joppa/Tarshish.

Joppa

Jonah traveled by boat/camel.

God/Jonah's conscience told him to go to Nineveh.

A fish/whale swallowed Jonah.

Jonah was thrown into jail/the sea.

Tarshish

When he got to land, he promised to obey God/quit sailing.

Inside the fish, Jonah slept/prayed.

Nineveh

Joseph's Coat

Directions: Have the children look up the Bible verse printed on each section of the coat. Instruct the children to color that section the color found in the verse. If the verse has more than one color, use the first color mentioned.

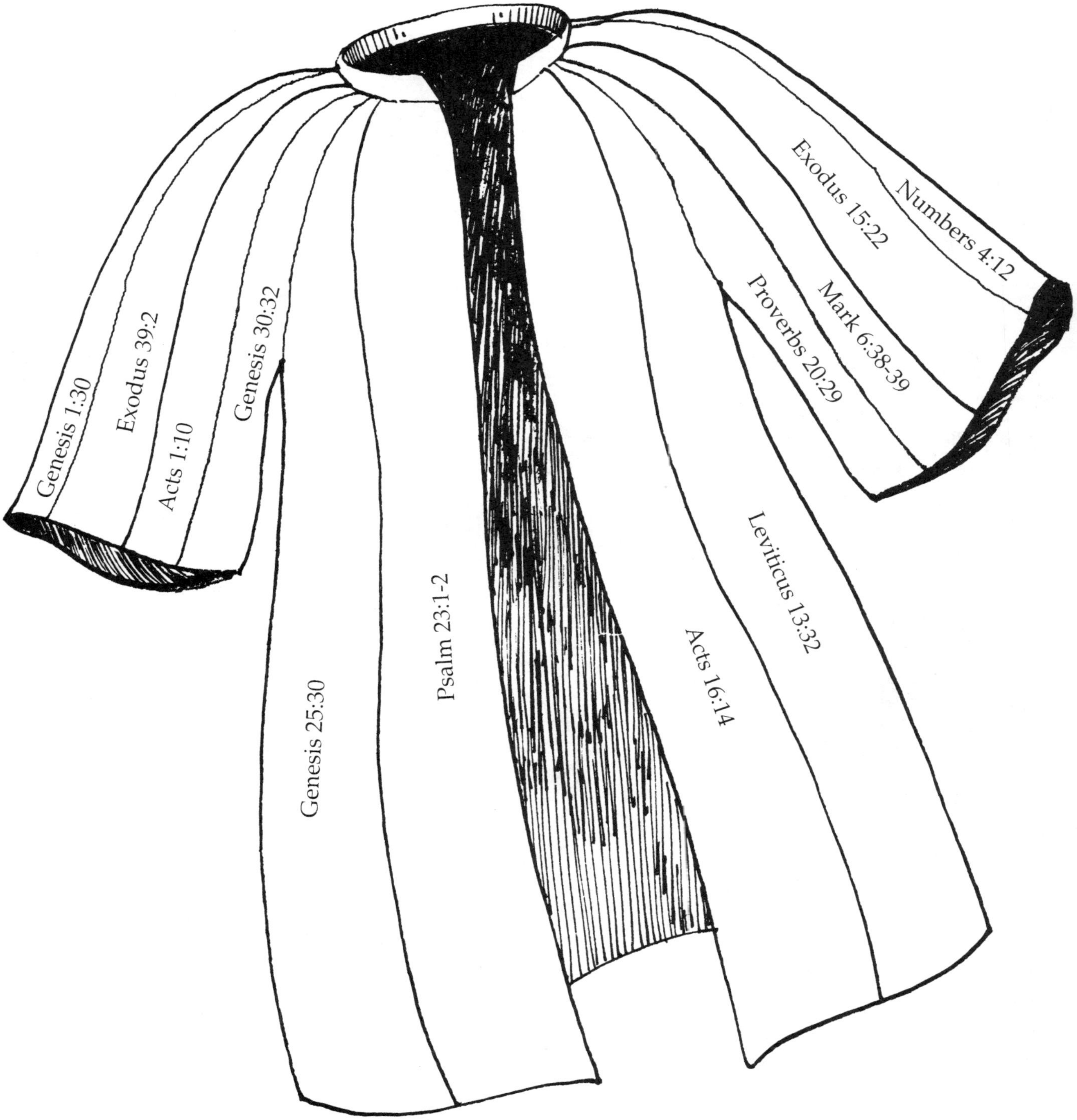

Genesis 1:30

Exodus 39:2

Acts 1:10

Genesis 30:32

Psalm 23:1-2

Genesis 25:30

Acts 16:14

Leviticus 13:32

Proverbs 20:29

Mark 6:38-39

Exodus 15:22

Numbers 4:12

© 1997 Abingdon Press
Art: Ron Hester © 1988 Graded Press

Find Joseph's Brothers

Directions: Have the children find Joseph's eleven brothers in the picture.

© 1997 Abingdon Press • Art: Michael Palan

58

ings

David and Solomon

Word game
1 Kings 2:2-3

Answers—page 60

BE STRONG, BE
COURAGEOUS, AND
KEEP THE CHARGE
OF THE LORD
YOUR GOD.

1 Kings 2:2b-3a

David and Solomon

Directions: Have the children write the letter that matches each crown in the space provided. Have the children check their answers by reading 1 Kings 2:2-3.

1 Kings 2:2b-3a

Lost Coin

The Lost Coin

Hidden picture
Luke 15:8-10

Lydia

Lydia

Coloring picture
Acts 16:11-15

The Lost Coin

Directions: Have the children find the coin hidden in the picture.

Lydia

Directions: Let the children decorate the picture with purple crayons.

# Martha

Martha
Matching cards
John 12:1-8

# Mary Magdalene

Mary Magdalene
Rebus puzzle
John 20:1-18

# Moses

Brave Women Who Helped Moses
Word search
Exodus 1:15-17; 2:5, 21; Numbers 26:59

God's Promise
Word game
Exodus 4:15

The Plagues of Egypt
Unscramble the words
Exodus 7:20-21; 8:5-6, 17, 21-24; 9:2-3, 10,
22-26; 10:13-14, 22; 12:29

Answers—page 68

```
S  S  I  U  Y  ●  S  I  S  T  Y  ●  P  H  A  R  M  I  R  I  J
M  I  H  W  I  F  J  O  C  V  J  O  C  H  E  B  E  D  O  ●  P
J  M  R  I  A  O  ●  P  R  Z  I  W  R  E  S  C  Z  I  P  P  M
●  I  M  I  P  J  O  E  J  O  C  I  S  H  I  P  U  A  Z  I  P
L  D  A  U  G  H  T  E  R  ●  O  F  ●  P  H  A  R  A  O  H  P
I  W  O  ●  S  S  R  P  U  A  Z  E  S  I  S  E  ●  T  A  E  R
M  I  O  T  I  T  Y  A  ●  I  P  H  R  ●  S  J  O  R  M  M  I
I  V  E  S  Z  I  P  U  H  D  A  U  G  C  P  H  O  R  I  H  A
S  E  S  I  S  M  A  I  R  I  M  ●  U  M  I  P  W  I  O  T  H
I  S  I  S  T  E  P  U  ●  I  U  E  P  H  P  U  J  O  H  B  E
●  J  O  C  ●  H  E  B  M  I  R  R  E  I  S  A  R  ●  C  U
S  H  ●  I  P  P  U  ●  A  I  P  U  Z  S  I  H  M  O  R  E  ●
```

Answers—page 70

Scramble	Answer	Reference
OODBL	Blood	Exodus 10:13-14
SFORG	Frogs	Exodus 9:2-3
STNAG	Gnats	Exodus 12:29
IESLF	Flies	Exodus 7:20-21
EPETSNICLE	Pestilence	Exodus 8:17
IOSLB	Boils	Exodus 10:22
IALH	Hail	Exodus 8:5-6
SSCLTUO	Locusts	Exodus 8:21-24
DRANKSSE	Darkness	Exodus 9:22-26
HAETD	Death	Exodus 9:10

Martha

Directions: Photocopy and cut apart at least two sets of the pictures. Let the children match the pictures.

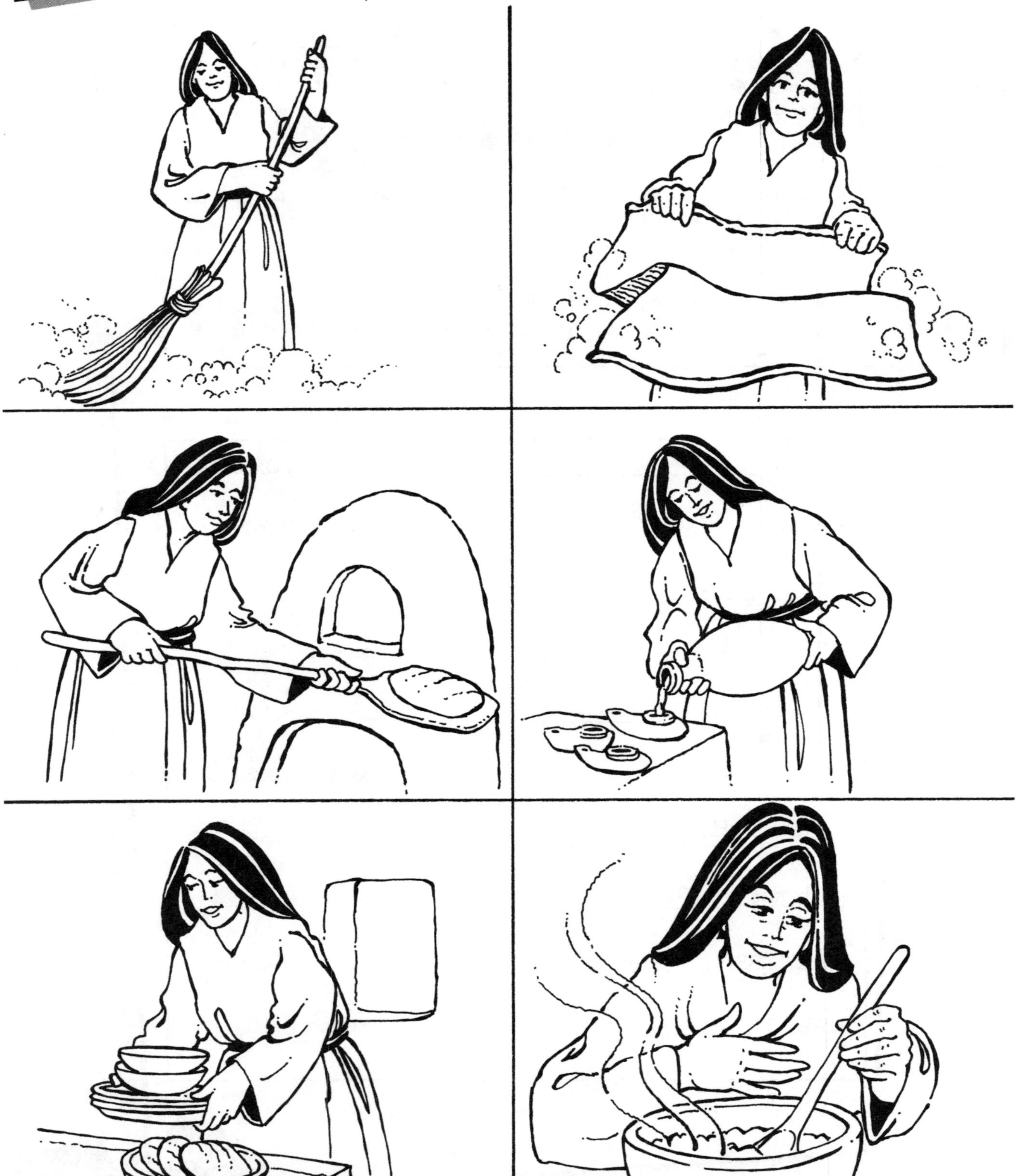

Mary Magdalene

Directions: Let the children solve the rebus puzzle.

Jesus [sled] -L **2** HER, "DO [scarf] [hotdog]+D on **2** ME, [bee]+Cause [eye] have [knot] YES-S+T ascended **2** the FARTHER-R [butter]-ER **GO 2** m+[eye] BOTHERS+R **&** say **2** THE+m, [eye] [ham]-H ASCENDING **2** M+[eye] FARTHER-R **&** YOU+r FARTHER-R, **2** m+[eye] God **&** YOU+R God.'" [people]-R Magdalene WENT **&** announced **2** the DIS+[eye]+PLES, "[eye] HAVE [bacon]+N the LORD."

© 1996 Cokesbury • Art: Robert S. Jones

67

Brave Women Who Helped Moses

Directions: Have the children look up the scriptures to find the names of women who helped Moses. Then have the children find the names in the word search.

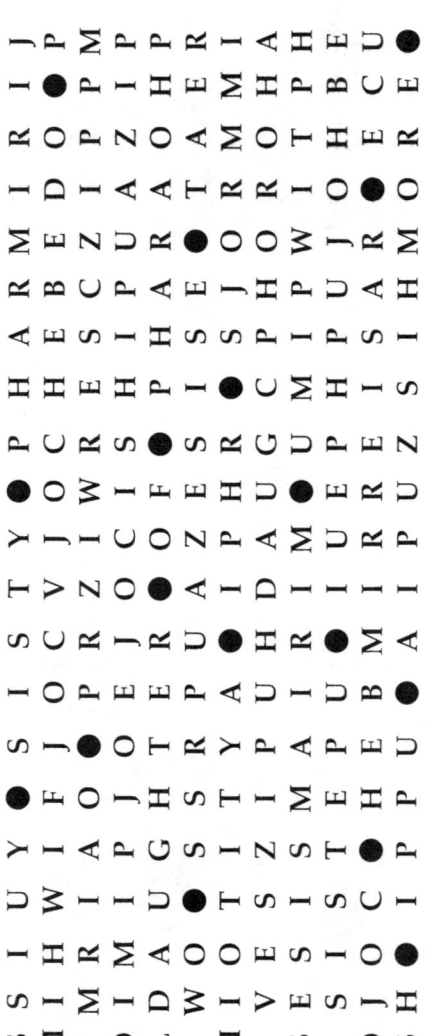

Brave Women Who Helped Moses

Find the names of some brave women and their relationship to Moses in the word search. Use your Bible to help you remember their names.

Two midwives — Exodus 1:15-17
Moses' mother and sister — Numbers 26:59
Moses' rescuer — Exodus 2:5
Moses' wife — Exodus 2:21

```
S S I U Y ● S I S T Y ● P H A R M I R I J
M I H W I F J O C V J O C H E B E D O ● P
J M R I A ● P R Z I W R E S C Z I P P M
● I M I P J O E J O C I S H I P U A Z I P
L D A U G H T E R ● O F P H A R A O H P
I W O ● S S R P U A Z E S I S E ● T A E R
M I O T I T Y A ● I P H R S J O R M M I
I V E S Z I P U H D A U G C P H O R O H A
S E S I S M A I R I M ● U M I P W I T P H
I S I S T E P U ● I U E P H P U J O H B E
● J O C ● H E B M I R R E I S A R ● E C U
S H ● I P P U ● A I P U Z S I H M O R E ●
```

68

God's Promise

Directions: Have the children write the letter that corresponds to the number under each space.

God's Promise

God said to Moses:

" ___ ___ ___ ___ ___   ___ ___   ___ ___ ___ ___
  9   23 9 12 12   2 5   23 9 20 8

___ ___ ___ ___   ___ ___ ___ ___ ___   ___ ___ ___
25 15 21 18   13 15 21 20 8   1 14 4

___ ___ ___ ___ ___   ___ ___ ___   ___ ___ ___ ___
20 5 1 3 8   25 15 21   23 8 1 20

___ ___ ___   ___ ___ ___   ___ ___
25 15 21   1 18 5   20 15

___ ___ ___ ___ ___."
19 16 5 1 11

A B C D E F G H I J K L M N O P Q R S T
1 2 3 4 5 6 7 8 9 10 11 12 13 14 15 16 17 18 19 20

U V W X Y Z
21 22 23 24 25 26

The Plagues of Egypt

Directions: Have the children unscramble the words to identify the plagues. Then have the children look up the Bible references and draw a line from the plague to the correct Bible verse.

The Israelites needed God's help! Pharaoh was not willing for them to leave Egypt. He did not want to obey God. As a result, God sent plagues to convince Pharaoh.

OODBL _____   Exodus 10:13-14

SFORG _____   Exodus 9:2-3

STNAG _____   Exodus 12:29

IESLF _____   Exodus 7:20-21

EPETSNICLE _____   Exodus 8:17

IOSLB _____   Exodus 10:22

IALH _____   Exodus 8:5-6

SSCLTUO _____   Exodus 8:21-24

DRANKSSE _____   Exodus 9:22-26

HAETD _____   Exodus 9:10

Nehemiah

Help Nehemiah
Maze
Nehemiah 1:1–2:6, 11-20

Noah

Noah's Ark
Coloring picture
Genesis 6:14-22

Rainbow Promise
Coloring picture
Genesis 9:12-17

Two by Two
Maze
Genesis 6:14-22

Help Nehemiah

Directions: Have the children follow the path around the city through the maze of the broken down city wall. The maze starts and ends at the same place.

Noah's Ark

Directions: Let the children decorate the picture with crayons or markers.

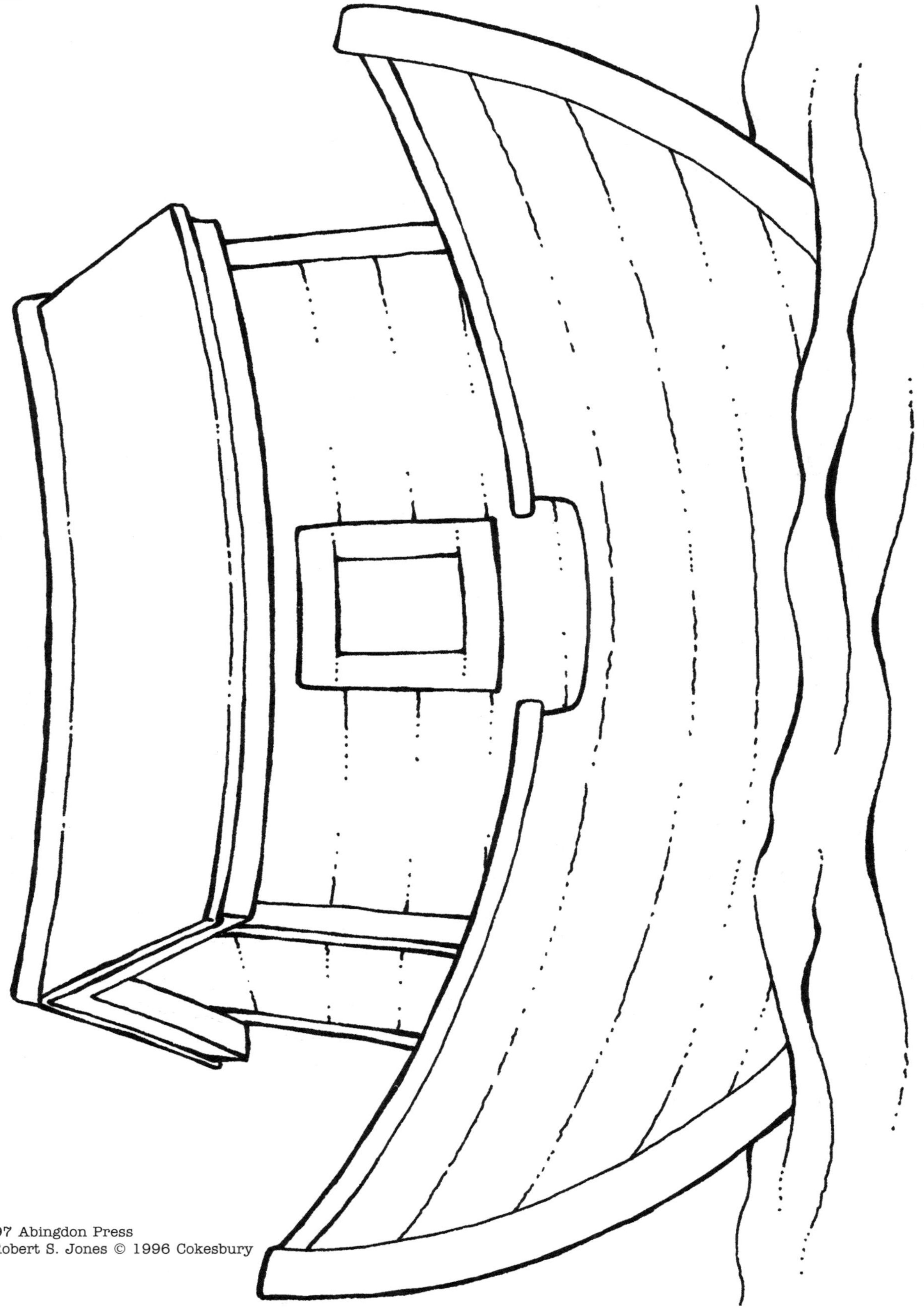

Rainbow Promise

Directions: Let the children decorate the picture with crayons or markers.

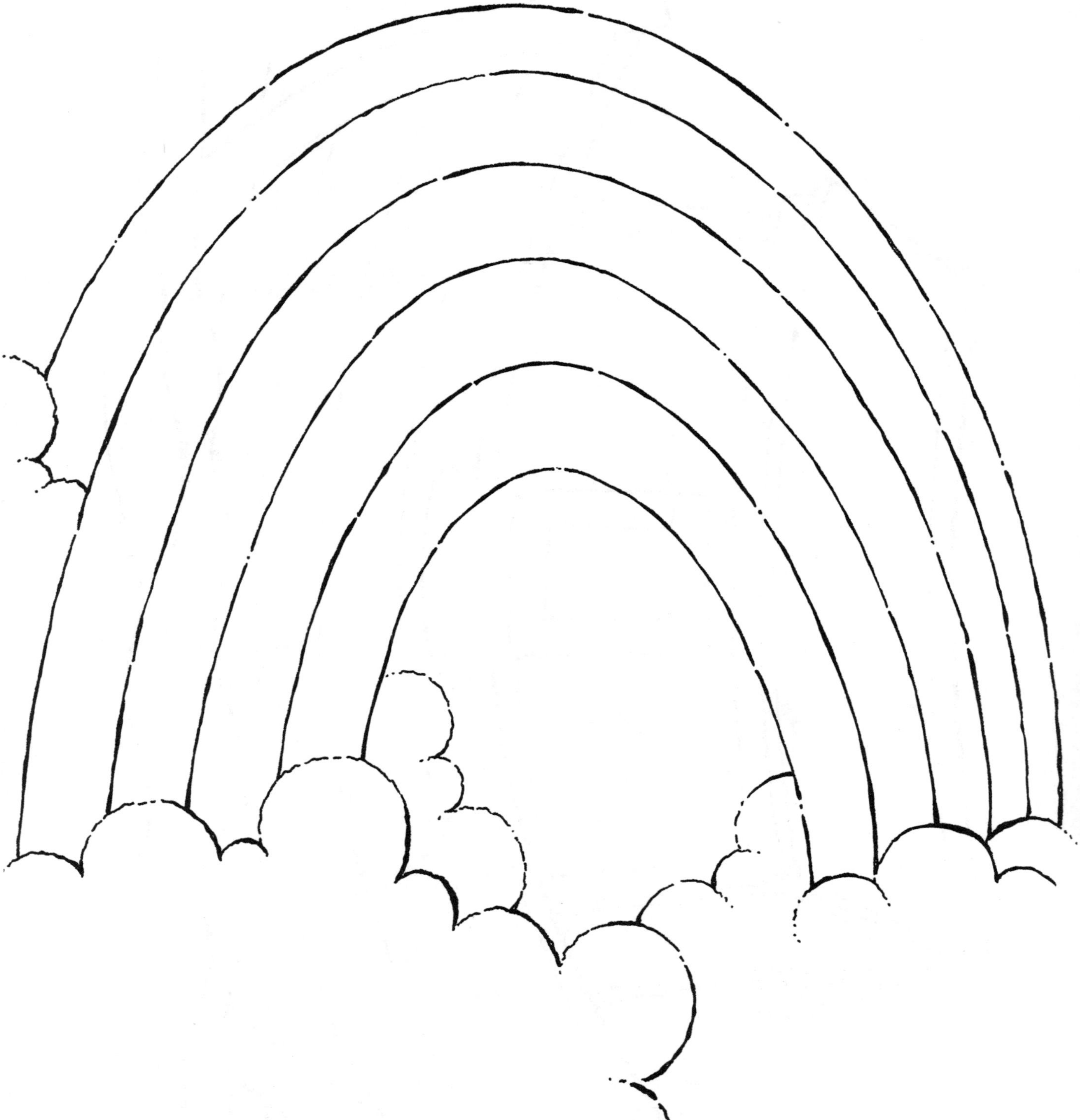

Two by Two

Directions: Have the children trace the path from each pair of animals to the ark.

Obed

Baby Obed
Coloring picture
Ruth 4:13-22

Baby Obed

Directions: Let the children decorate the picture with crayons or markers.
Have pieces of tissue paper or strips of gauze. Let the children glue the tissue
paper or gauze onto their pictures to make baby Obed's swaddling clothes.

© 1998 Abingdon Press • Art: Robert S. Jones

77

Paul

Tentmakers
Dot-to-dot picture
Acts 18:1-3

Paul
Word search
Acts 10:34

Answers—page 80

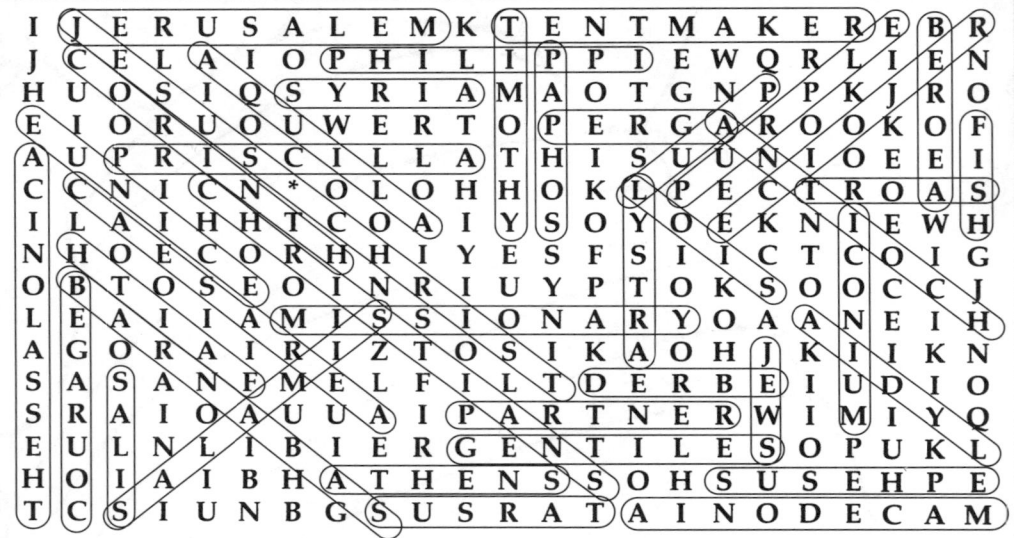

Prayer

Hear My Prayer
Fill in the blanks
Psalm 4:1c; 42:8; Matthew 21:22; Luke 6:12;
Romans 12:12; Ephesians 6:18; Philippians 1:9-10

Pray at All Times
Coloring page
Romans 12:12

Tentmakers

Directions: Have the children connect the dots to complete the tent. Then trace the dots to finish Paul's letter.

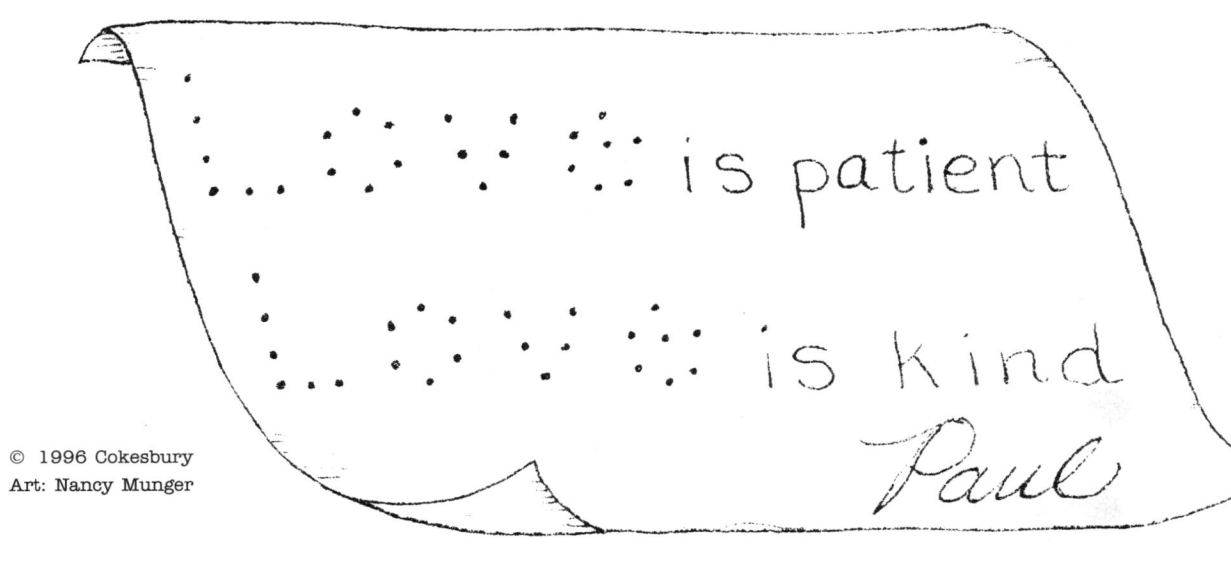

is patient

is kind

Paul

79

Paul

Directions: Have the children find the words listed under people, places, and other important words.

```
I J E R U S A L E M K T E N T M A K E R E B R
J C E L A I O P H I L I P P I E W Q R L I E N
H U O S I Q S Y R I A M A O T G N P P K J R O
E I O R U O U W E R T O P E R G A R O O K O F
A U P R I S C I L L A T H I S U U N I O E E I
C C N I C N * O L O H H O K L P E C T R O A S
I L A I H H T C O A I Y S O Y O E K N I E W H
N H O E C O R H H I Y E S F S I I C T C O I G
O B T O S E O I N R I U Y P T O K S O O C C J
L E A I I A M I S S I O N A R Y O A A N E I H
A G O R A I R I Z T O S I K A O H J K I I K N
S A S A N F M E L F I L T D E R B E I U D I O
S R A I O A U U A I P A R T N E R W I M I Y Q
E U L N L I B I E R G E N T I L E S O P U K L
H O I A I B H A T H E N S S O H S U S E H P E
T C S I U N B G S U S R A T A I N O D E C A M
```

People
Aquila
Barnabas
Eunice
Jesus Christ
Lois
Lydia
Paul
Priscilla
Silas
Timothy

Places
Antioch
Athens
Beroea
Caesarea
Corinth
Derbe
Ephesus
Iconium
Jerusalem
Lystra
Macedonia
Paphos
Perga
Philippi
Salamis
Syria
Tarsus
Thessalonica
Troas

Other Important Words
Christians
Courage
Faith
Fish
Gentiles
Jews
Missionary
Purple
Tentmaker
Partner
Rejoice

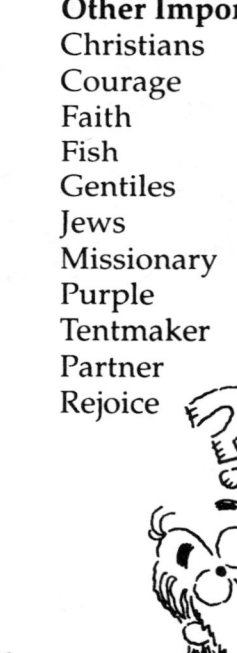

80

Hear My Prayer

Directions: Have the children look up the Scripture passages to fill in the blanks.

Look up these Scripture passages on prayer and fill in the blanks. When you have finished, you may want to write your own prayer on the back of your paper.

Be _____ to me and hear my prayer. (Psalm 4:1c)

By day the Lord commands his _____ _____, and at night his song is with me, a _____ to the God of my life. (Psalm 42:8)

"Whatever you ask for in prayer with _____, you will _____." (Matthew 21:22)

Now during those days he went out to the _____ to pray; and he spent the _____ in prayer to God. (Luke 6:12)

_____ in hope, be _____ in suffering, persevere in prayer. (Romans 12:12)

Pray in the _____ at all times in every prayer and _____. (Ephesians 6:18)

And this is my prayer, that your _____ may _____ more and more with knowledge and full _____ to help you to determine what is best. (Philippians 1:9-10)

Pray at All Times

Directions: Let the children decorate the picture with crayons or markers.

Pray at all times.

Romans 12:12,
Good News Bible

© 1997 Abingdon Press • Art: Robert S. Jones

QueEN Esther

Queen Esther

Coloring page

Esther 1:1—10:3

Queen Esther

Directions: Let the children decorate the picture with crayons or markers.

Ruth

Ruth and Naomi

Word search
Ruth 1:1—4:22

Answers—page 86

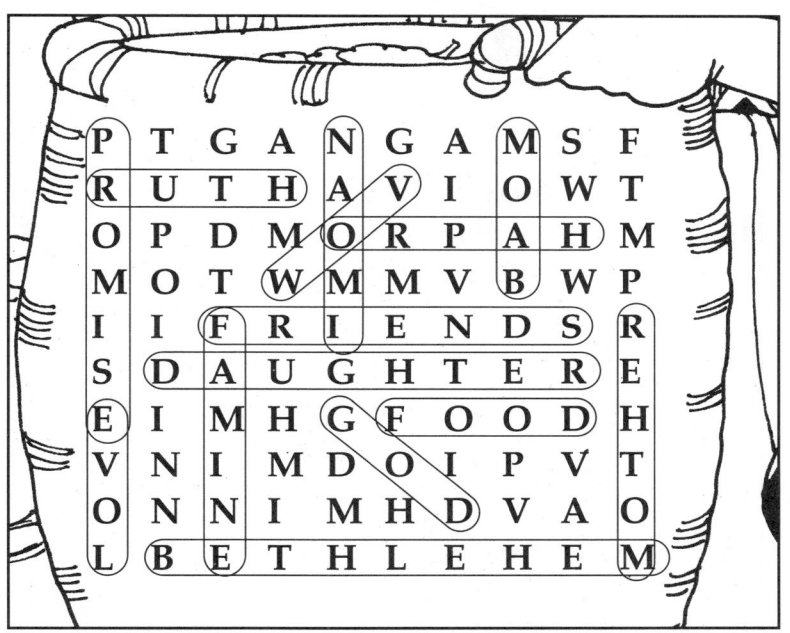

P T G A N G A M S F
R U T H A V I O W T
O P D M O R P A H M
M O T W M M V B W P
I I F R I E N D S R
S D A U G H T E R E
E I M H G F O O D H
V N I M D O I P V T
O N N I M H D V A O
L B E T H L E H E M

Ruth and Naomi

Directions: Have the children find the words from the word list in the word puzzle.

Word List

Bethlehem   Love
Daughter   Moab
Famine   Mother
Food   Naomi
Friends   Orpah
God   Ruth
Promise
Vow

P T G A N G A M S F
R U T H A V I O W T
O P D M O R P A H M
M O T W M M V B W P
I I F R I E N D S R
S D A U G H T E R E
E I M H G F O O D H
V N I M D O I P V T
O N N I M H D V A O
L B E T H L E H E M

ShepherdS

Shepherds on the Hillside
Coloring page
Luke 2:8-20

Shepherds
Maze
Psalm 23

Shepherds on the Hillside

Directions: Let the children decorate the picture with crayons or markers.
Let the children add star stickers to the sky.

© 1997 Abingdon Press • Art: Robert S. Jones

Shepherds

Directions: Have the children trace the paths from each shepherd to each finish line.

START

FINISH

START

FINISH

Ten Commandments

I Will Serve the Lord
Word game
Exodus 20:1-17

Thinking of You

Jesus Loves You!
Greeting card

Thinking About You
Greeting card

90

I Will Serve the Lord

Directions: Have the children write one of the Ten Commandments in their own words on each of the rocks in the altar.

The people of Israel promised to serve God. They promised to remember the Ten Commandments and to obey God's law. Do you remember the Ten Commandments?

1

2   3   4

5   6   7

8   9   10

Jesus Loves You!

Directions: Have the children decorate the cards with crayons or markers.
Send the cards to persons in your church as thinking-of-you cards.

Jesus loves you!

Thinking About You

Directions: Have the children decorate the cards with crayons or markers.
Send the cards to persons in your church as thinking-of-you cards.

I've been thinking about you

and I have been praying for you.

Upper Room

The Upper Room

Crossword puzzle
Mark 14:16-25; John 13:34

Answers—page 95

The Upper Room

Directions: Have the children use their Bibles to answer the questions and complete the crossword puzzle.

ACROSS

4 and 5. The two disciples were sent to the
   city to prepare the _____ _____.
      (Mark 14:16)
6. Jesus took a loaf of bread and said, "Take.
   This is my _____."   (Mark 14:22)
7. "I will never again drink of the fruit of the
   _____ until that day when I drink it new
in the kingdom of God."   (Mark 14:25)
9. Jesus gave the disciples a new _____.
      (John 13:34)

DOWN

1. Jesus blessed and broke the _____.
      (Mark 14:22)
2. "_____ one another."   (John 13:34)
3. Christians celebrate _____ _____
   with bread and wine or juice.
6. "This is my _____ of the covenant."
      (Mark 14:24)
8. Jesus broke the bread after _____ it.
      (Mark 14:22)

If you need help, find the answers in your Bible.

Vineyard

I Am the Vine

Coloring page
John 15:5

I Am the Vine

Directions: Have the children decorate the picture with crayons or markers.

*I am
the vine,
you are the
branches.*

John 15:5

Wise Men

Gifts for the King
Coloring picture
Matthew 2:1-12

Follow the Star
Maze
Matthew 2:1-12

Star Code
Word game
Matthew 2:1-12

The Wise Men
Fact search
Matthew 2:1-12

Woman at the Well

Woman at the Well
Coloring picture
John 4: 1-42

World

God So Loved the World
Coloring poster
John 3:16

98

Gifts for the King

Directions: Let the children decorate the picture with crayons or markers.

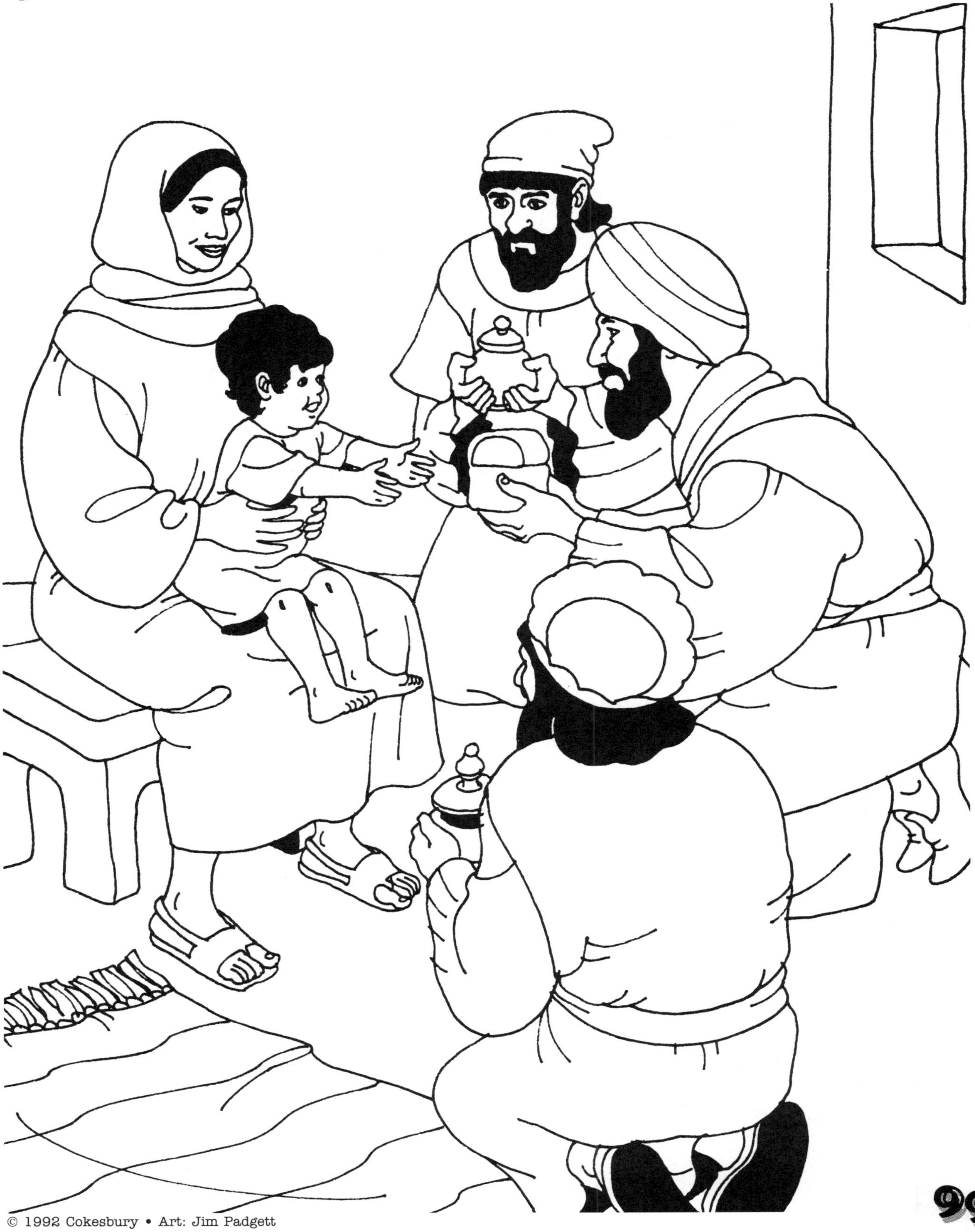

99

Follow the Star

Directions: Have the children trace the path from the wise men to Bethlehem. Then have the children trace the path the wise men took from Bethlehem back home.

The East

Bethlehem

© 1997 Abingdon Press • Art: Larry Rollins

100

Star Code

Directions: Have the children use the star code to find out more about the visit of the wise men. Check answers in Matthew 2:1-12.

Wise men, having seen a _____, came from the _____ to _____ looking for the king of the _____.

King _____ was frightened. He asked the chief priests and scribes where the _____ was to be born. They answered, "In _____ of Judea."

When the wise men found Jesus, they were _____ with _____. They worshiped Jesus and gave him gifts of _____, _____, and _____.

Being warned in a dream not to return to Herod, the wise men returned home by another road.

A-☆ D-☆ G-☆ J-☆ M-☆ O-☆ R-☆ U-☆ X-☆
B-☆ E-☆ H-☆ K-☆ N-☆ P-☆ S-☆ V-☆ Y-★
C-☆ F-☆ I-☆ L-☆   Q-☆ T-☆ W-☆ Z-☆

The Wise Men

Directions: Let the children read Matthew 2:1-12 and then place a check mark beside each fact that we can learn about the wise men from the Bible.

Matthew is the only gospel that tells the story of the wise men from the East. However, the biblical story tells us very little about them. Most of the ideas we have about these wise men come from stories that have become a part of our tradition.

___ 1. Came from the East.

___ 2. Had seen a star.

___ 3. Found the baby Jesus in a manger.

___ 4. Rode camels.

___ 5. Were looking for the King of the Jews.

___ 6. Traveled at night.

___ 7. Were astrologers.

___ 8. Came to pay homage to Jesus.

___ 9. Traveled in a group of three.

___10. Came from three different countries.

___11. Were told that the Messiah was to be born in Bethlehem.

___12. Said something that frightened King Herod.

___13. Were led by a star.

___14. Brought gifts of gold, frankincense, and myrrh.

___15. Were named Caspar, Balthazar, and Melchior.

___16. Were warned in a dream not to return to Herod.

___17. Were happy when they found Jesus.

___18. Went home by a different route than the route they had come.

Were they Kings? Perhaps. Maybe that idea comes from Psalm 68:29 and Psalm 72:10 that speak of kings bearing gifts.

How many? They brought three gifts, but there could have been two or even twelve wise men!

Where did they find Jesus? Jesus' family was in a house by now. Jesus may have been as much as two years old.

Were they astrologers? Maybe. The Greek word that Matthew uses to describe them is *magi*. That identifies them as priests. Perhaps they were astrologers too.

Woman at the Well

Directions: Let the children decorate the picture with crayons or markers.

God So Loved the World

Directions: Let the children decorate the poster with crayons or markers.

God so loved the world

John 3:16

XPICTOC

XPICTOC (Chi Rho)

Monogram

XPICTOC (Chi Rho)

Directions: Have the children decorate the monogram for Christ with crayons, markers, or glitter pens.

The word *Christ* in Greek is *XPICTOC* (pronounced Christos). The first two letters, XP, form this symbol. It is called the Chi Rho (pronounced Ky Ro).

Yahweh

Names for God
Word search

Answers—page 108

```
A Y T S E J A M B S I R F G
E I A C J L A G Y A H W E H
D H Y H F X V T G O D J Z L
W X O X W J E H O V A H S O
G N I K K E B U D M Y H C R
V Q T E Y A H W E H N E A D
H Y A R U W M A S K O W H L
C R E A T O R X Q P Z H A K
D X Y V N B M H E W H A Y C
V O L O R D Y X V G K Y X C
```

Directions: Have the children find the names for God from the list in the word puzzle.

Yahweh
God
Lord
Majesty
Creator
King
Jehovah

A Y T S E J A M B S I R F G
E I A C J L A G Y A H W E H
D H Y H F X V T G O D J Z L
W X O X W J E H O V A H S O
G N I K K E B U D M Y H C R
V Q T E Y A H W E H N E A D
H Y A R U W M A S K O W H L
C R E A T O R X Q P Z H A K
D X Y V N B M H E W H A Y C
V O L O R D Y X V G K Y X C

Zacchaeus

What Can You Find in the Tree?
Hidden Picture
Luke 19:1-9

Zacchaeus, Come Down!
Coloring Picture
Luke 19:1-9

What Can You Find in the Tree?

Directions: Have the children find the pictures hidden in the tree.

© 1997 Abingdon Press • Art: Michael Palan

Zacchaeus, Come Down!

Directions: Let the children enjoy coloring the picture of Zacchaeus.

Index